PREVENTION'S

Healthy
WEEKNIGHT
MEALS
In Minutes

Edited by David Joachim, *PREVENTION* Magazine Health Books

Rodale Press, Inc.
Emmaus, Pennsylvania

This book is simultaneously being published by Rodale Press as *Prevention's Quick and Healthy Low-Fat Cooking: Featuring Weeknight Meals in Minutes.*

Copyright © 1997 by Rodale Press, Inc.
Illustrations copyright © 1997 by Sara Swan
Photographs copyright © 1997 by Rodale Press, Inc.

Front Cover: Pinto Bean Chili (page 32) and
Jalapeño Buttermilk Cornbread (page 31)

Cover Photography: Tad Ware & Company, Inc.

Library of Congress Cataloging-in-Publication Data

Prevention's healthy weeknight meals in minutes / edited by David
    Joachim, food editor ; Prevention Magazine Health Books.
        p.   cm.
    Hardback ed. published simultaneously as: Prevention's quick and
healthy low-fat cooking: featuring weeknight meals in minutes.
    Includes index.
    ISBN 0–87596–370–6 paperback
    1. Low-fat diet—Recipes.   I. Joachim, David.   II. Prevention
Magazine Health Books.   III. Prevention's quick and healthy low-fat
cooking.
RM237.7.P738   1996
641.5'638—dc20   96–35997

        2   4   6   8   10   9   7   5   3   1   paperback

_____ OUR PURPOSE _____
*"We inspire and enable people to improve
their lives and the world around them."*
_____ RODALE ⚜ BOOKS _____

Prevention's Healthy Weeknight Meals in Minutes
Editorial Staff

Editor: David Joachim
Managing Editor: Jean Rogers
Contributing Writer: Mary Carroll
Researchers and Fact-Checkers: Sandra Salera Lloyd,
Michelle Szulborski Zenie
Book and Cover Designer: Debra Sfetsios
Design Coordinator: Darlene Schneck
Studio Manager: Joe Golden
Book Layout: Tad Ware & Company, Inc.
Illustrator: Sara Swan
Photographer: Tad Ware Photography
Food Stylist: Robin Krause
Recipe Development: Mary Carroll
Nutritional Consultants: Linda Yoakam, M.S., R.D.; Anita Hirsch, R.D.
Director, Book Manufacturing: Helen Clogston
Manufacturing Coordinator: Melinda B. Rizzo

Prevention *Magazine Health Books*

Vice-President and Editorial Director: Debora T. Yost
Art Director: Jane Colby Knutila
Research Manager: Ann Gossy Yermish
Copy Manager: Lisa D. Andruscavage

Contents

Introduction

You can't beat home-cooked meals. They're less expensive and healthier than going out, and they bring the family together. More than any other time in the past ten years, people are reaping the benefits of cooking at home. A Better Homes and Gardens study showed that most Americans eat home-cooked meals five to six nights a week.

But we're also busier than ever. According to the U.S. Department of Agriculture, most of us decide what's for dinner only four hours before it's time to eat. And half of all working adults eat lunch at their desks. Let's face it: At the end of a long day, the last thing you want to do is worry about dinner.

We've designed this book to put healthy dinners on your table night after night—without a minute's thought. We show you how to cut shopping time and what to keep on hand for quick weeknight meals that you can feel good about. When you get home from work, just pick a dinner and follow the simple game plan. Dinner will be on the table in 45 minutes or less.

You'll even find tips for eating smart away from home. Want to know the healthiest fast-food chains? How to get a nutritious airplane meal? How to pack low-fat lunches for you and your kids? The top 20 healthy snacks? It's all here.

Today's busy families need good food without a lot of fuss. With this book you can have healthy burgers, chili, turkey pot pie, macaroni and cheese, chocolate snack cake—all your everyday favorites—in minutes. The best part is, you'll have more time to enjoy your meals. And that's what good food is all about.

David Joachim
Prevention Magazine Health Books

CHAPTER 1

FAST, NO-FUSS
WAYS TO
UPGRADE YOUR
EATING

STAYING HEALTHY IN A BUSY WORLD

Eating has evolved from a simple life-sustaining activity into our national preoccupation. And also our national worry. Because we think we don't have time to eat well.

In this accelerated society, the days of browsing the supermarket and endless time to cook have been replaced by browsing the Internet and endless deadlines. We skip fresh in pursuit of fast and see less of our kitchens than our computers. We manage to slap together a peanut butter sandwich or dial out for pizza between faxes, and we consider ourselves fed.

Anyone with the least amount of health awareness can get very discouraged scanning daily newspaper stories. One

1

scientific study after another reveals something new to avoid: red meat, cheese, butter, alcohol, salt, too many refined foods. Our icons, like olive oil or oat bran, come under attack and sometimes fall.

We look for a way to get back to home-cooked meals—something that will sustain us and satisfy both body and soul. But the boss calls a late meeting and it's one more night of fast food or microwave popcorn.

What if we were to tell you that you *can* have dinner on the table— a weeknight meal that's delicious, a hit with the family and healthy to boot—before the pizza guy rings your doorbell? We're not talking five-page gourmet recipes with long lists of specialized ingredients. We're talking simple, good-tasting food. And the techniques to prepare it fast and healthy.

Cooking at home is the only sure way to control what we eat. Home-cooked meals are usually healthier and lower in fat than takeout or restaurant meals. We can monitor the freshness of ingredients and the nutritional variety—components of well-being and good health. And if you know the ropes, cooking healthy takes no more time than waiting for that pizza or heating up a frozen TV dinner. The secret is shopping smart, buying quick-cooking ingredients and planning ahead. These are the keys to healthy weeknight meals that won't put a cramp in your busy lifestyle.

TAKE CONTROL OF YOUR EATING

Cooking quick, energy-rich meals for yourself and your family is a health priority; just like getting enough sleep or exercise. In these busy times, you need to keep your body at peak condition just to fight fatigue and illness.

Fear of fat has led many of us astray, say nutritionists. We stock up on low-nutrient fat-free convenience foods and ignore fresh, well-balanced meals. Just using a lot of no-fat and low-fat ingredients doesn't equal instant nutrition. That's oversimplifying the facts, and it could be dangerous to your health, according to Michele Tuttle, M.P.H., R.D., director of consumer affairs at the Food Marketing Institute in Washington, D.C. If you focus too much on cutting out fat by eating fat-free packaged foods, you'll probably miss or unbalance other important nutrients, like iron, zinc, beta-carotene, folic acid and vitamins A, C, D and E. And many fat-free convenience foods have extra calories and salt to make up for lack of taste.

"This is why as a nation we're getting fatter even though we're eating fat-free products," says Susan G. Purdy, author of *Have Your Cake and Eat It, Too* and *Let Them Eat Cake*. If you cook a variety of foods and cut back on fat—not eliminate it—you won't be making the severe taste trade-offs that lead to failure with healthy eating. You'll love your food, and you'll love the way you feel.

We all know that taste is tops. Despite our good intentions, we won't stick with healthy eating long-term unless it also tastes great. "So my rule in making healthy meals is: appetizing first, healthy second," says Martha Rose Shulman, award-winning author of *Provençal Light*, *Mediterranean Light* and *Mexican Light*. Shulman keeps her kitchen stocked with foods that inspire her to cook this way: quality fresh foods that cook fast. "What you have on hand, you'll use," she says. "Beautiful, quick-cooking ingredients make you gravitate toward beautiful, quick-cooking meals."

Stocking up on the right ingredients is just one of the kitchen shortcuts cooking experts employ to create healthy meals in a matter of minutes. But the big timesaver is planning, says Brenda Ponichtera, R.D., author of *Quick & Healthy Recipes and Ideas* and *Quick & Healthy Volume II*. "Gathering recipes that don't take long to prepare and that your family enjoys is the first step. Then plan menus around these recipes. When my patients take time to plan, their week is so much easier." We know you're pressed for time. So we've taken that first step for you. All you need to do is pick a dinner from the more than 100 menus provided here.

START HEALTHY, STAY HEALTHY

Plan on starting your morning with energy-rich foods. A healthy breakfast means good self-esteem and energy all day long, says Elizabeth Somer, R.D., author of *Food and Mood*. Skipping breakfast can lead to fatigue and mood swings later in the day. "This is especially important for women, who are always dieting. They often skip breakfast, then they have uncontrollable cravings later in the day," says Somer. Take five minutes to eat something quick and healthy for breakfast.

What you eat in the morning creates a foundation of health you build on the rest of the day. Even a glass of fruit juice and a glass of skim milk will sustain you longer than a sweet roll or a low-cal breakfast bar, says Evelyn Tribole, M.S., R.D., a nutritionist in private practice in Beverly Hills, California, and author of *Healthy Homestyle Cooking*.

Many of us skip breakfast because we've fallen into an eating rut and need to expand our culinary horizons, says Susan Asanovic, M.S., R.D., owner of the food and nutrition consulting firm La Table Dans Le Bon Sens in Wilton, Connecticut. Vary your diet. Try a quick new fruit, like papaya ("a nutritional superstar," says Asanovic), or a new cereal for breakfast. You can even pack along your own take-out breakfast—a low-fat burrito or leftover pasta from dinner—to eat later at the office. That'll begin satisfying your body's morning nutritional needs and build resources for all-day energy.

What about those super-rushed days when breakfast is small and lunch preempted by nonstop work? Count on afternoon snacks and dinner to fill in the nutritious foods you missed, says Anita Hirsch, M.S., R.D., nutritionist at Rodale Press, Inc. and staff nutritionist for *Quick and Healthy Cooking* magazine. When you're eating in a hurry, up the value of everything you eat with nutrient-dense foods. Cruciferous vegetables, soyfoods like tofu and complex carbohydrates like brown rice can do wonders for your health, according to Nan Kathryn Fuchs, Ph.D., a nutritionist in private practice in Sebastopol, California, nutrition editor of *Women's Health Letter*, and author of *Overcoming the Legacy of Overeating*. Dr. Fuchs's basic marinara sauce counteracts the stress of a hectic day with extra nutrition from carrots, chard and broccoli, which give it a rich flavor her family loves.

As you venture into this new approach to eating, you might need to reset your food attitudes. Slow and steady is the key to lasting changes that build a good foundation of health, says Ponichtera. "Ask yourself, 'Can I switch from whole milk to 2 percent? Regular mayonnaise to reduced-fat?' If good-tasting lower-fat versions of your favorites are available, try them with an open mind. Try to make changes you can stick with. You may prefer the taste of low-fat products instead of fat-free products. And that's fine if it can be a permanent change."

GUIDELINES FOR GOOD HEALTH

Experts say that if you can change only two things about your diet, concentrate on lowering fat and adding fiber. This simple strategy will focus all your menu planning on the base of the USDA Food Guide Pyramid and gradually adjust your thinking of the typical dinner plate.

The Food Guide Pyramid illustrates for Americans the current scientific suggestions for healthy eating. At the top of the pyramid are the least-recommended foods—those to be eaten in smallest quantity, like fats, oils and sweets. At the base of the pyramid are the basic building blocks of nutrition needed to prevent chronic diseases like cancer, heart disease and diabetes. The pyramid redefines our priorities: eat mostly whole grains and cereals, plus fresh fruits and vegetables. Use less whole milk and meat to avoid saturated fats. Instead of the 8-ounce T-bone steak, you might serve 2 or 3 ounces of lean chicken or fish, with ½ cup cooked rice or couscous and steamed broccoli, plus 1 cup tossed salad with a low-fat dressing.

The USDA's *Healthy Eating Index*, which monitors how we eat, found that fewer than one out of five people eat the recommended five servings of fruits and vegetables per day. We're also missing out on the recommended amount of grains. Less than one-third of Americans have enough variety in their diets. Experts recommend eating 16 different food items over a three-day period. Less than 20 percent of us manage to cut saturated fats to 10 percent of total calories or to cut total fat intake to 30 percent or less—the recommended limits. And only 35 percent reduce their daily salt intake to 2,400 milligrams or less.

What does this say about our eating habits? Caught in the time trap, we rush past the best nutrient-rich foods, like fresh fruits and vegetables, grains and legumes, says Tuttle. "It just shows that we have a way to go in eating healthy. We're not eating according to the Food Guide Pyramid, and we need to move in that direction."

Five servings of fresh fruits and vegetables a day is surprisingly easy to get, says Asanovic. Just frequent salad bars and buy precut, prewashed lettuce, carrots, celery sticks and other produce. Stock up on fruit salad for lunch and greens and other vegetables to take home for dinner stir-fries or vegetable salads. The best supermarkets prep twice daily, so the items are fresh. To get the best possible ingredients, Asanovic recommends asking the manager of your favorite store which are the freshly prepared selections. Or buy bagged mesclun or other high-flavor lettuces and serve salad at each meal, suggests Faye Levy, author of *30 Low-Fat Meals in 30 Minutes*; everyone will eat more of the healthy vegetables and less of the higher-fat entrée.

Jeanne Jones, "Cook It Light" nationally syndicated columnist, starts getting her five-a-day with fruit for breakfast: favorites are grilled banana on toast ("which tastes like banana jam," says Jones) and frozen banana blended with skim milk over shredded wheat cereal.

For lunch and dinner get inspiration from other cultures—see how they incorporate vegetables into fast meals, says Dr. Fuchs. For example, Chinese vegetable lo mein is essentially pasta and fast-cooked fresh vegetables. Instead of having one large piece of meat as your main dish, try incorporating vegetables and meats in one dish like a pot pie, stir-fry or pasta with meat or seafood. Even a meal as simple as sautéed Swiss chard, dressed with lemon juice, capers and chopped sun-dried tomatoes over pasta, will get you closer to your five-a-day goal.

• **Pasta with Lean and Luscious Alfredo Sauce:** Puree cottage cheese with yogurt, garlic and Parmesan. Toss with steamed broccoli and pasta. To save time, cook the broccoli in the same water as the pasta, adding it a few minutes before the pasta is done. —From Martha Rose Shulman

• **Mexican Snack Night:** Top baked tortilla chips with warmed low-fat refried beans, shredded low-fat cheese and fat-free sour cream; serve with bowls of chopped avocado, broccoli, jicama and baby carrots. Set it up as a picnic on the living room floor—kids love this one. —From Elizabeth Somer

• **Adobo Chicken with Quinoa:** Marinate boneless skinless chicken breasts in chilies, lime juice and cumin, then grill and serve them over a quinoa pilaf made with onions, celery and garlic. —From Steven Raichlen

• **Tri-Pepper Pasta:** Sauté red, yellow and green bell peppers with plenty of garlic and a hint of olive oil and Parmesan. Serve over pasta. —From Evelyn Tribole

• **Catfish with Red Pepper Sauce:** Puree drained, jarred roasted red peppers with chicken broth. Serve over oven-fried catfish on a bed of steamed spinach. —From Coleen Miner

• **Chinese Feast Night:** Make chicken chop suey with frozen chicken breasts, celery, onions and canned bean sprouts. Serve over rice. —From Brenda Ponichtera

• **French Bread Pizza Dinner:** Top French bread with low-fat spaghetti sauce and shredded low-fat mozzarella cheese. Bake until the cheese melts. Serve with tossed salad, baby carrots and a low-fat dip made from cottage cheese or low-fat yogurt blended with an envelope of soup mix. —From Anne Fletcher

• **Moroccan Nights:** Toss cooked couscous with steamed vegetables and a low-fat vinaigrette dressing. —From Paulette Mitchell

STAYING HEALTHY AWAY FROM HOME

When you travel, all bets are off. Or are they? Can you eat healthy on the road, as well as on the run?

"People say to me, 'When I travel, I give up eating healthy; it just can't be done.' But I find it's not hard at all," says Tuttle. "Hotels offer skim milk, bagels, fresh fruit and cereals for breakfast. If you're having a full day of meetings with preset meals, take advantage of breakfast where you have control. Even at preset dinners you can ask for more salad, skim milk or healthy choices."

Consulting with nutritional clients all over the world keeps cookbook author and syndicated columnist Jeanne Jones's travel schedule pretty hectic. How does she manage to eat light in every port of call? It becomes a simple matter of learning what to look for on a variety of restaurant menus, Jones explains. Educate yourself to recognize lighter dishes. These include fresh green salads with low-fat dressing on the side; lean cuts of meat, poultry and fish that are baked or broiled without sauce; side dishes of steamed or stir-fried vegetables; baked potatoes; and simple fruit desserts. When scanning the menu at a restaurant, steer clear of dishes that sport *fried, deep-fried, cream sauce* and other high-fat indicators in the title. Instead, look for terms like *grilled, broiled, light, lean* and *low-fat*. You can even call ahead to see which healthy selections the restaurant offers. When we tested this theory, most chefs were quite willing to accommodate special requests—and show off their skill with fresh foods.

Some savvy travelers carry their own low-fat salad dressings, salt substitutes or sweetener in their bag or briefcase. Any restaurant can fix green salad without dressing, and you can request extra lemon wedges and vinegar and a tiny bit of oil on the side. Or as Jones does, you can dilute a half teaspoonful of dressing with lemon juice to get the flavor without much fat.

Another option experts use when traveling: book hotel rooms with a kitchenette or refrigerator to save on restaurant meals. Stock it with low-fat breakfast foods, fruit and whole-grain breads. Asanovic packs boxed tofu, whole-grain crackers and low-sodium cups of soup. She sometimes brings a cooler with yogurt, fruit, cut-up carrots and low-fat cheese to put in the hotel mini-bar refrigerator for snacking. As a last resort, especially if there are no accommodating restaurants in town, you can buy healthy sandwich fixings, a salad or fruit at the local market—and pack a picnic for the park or to eat in your hotel room.

Paulette Mitchell, a cooking instructor and consultant in Minneapolis, Minnesota, and author of *The Fifteen-Minute Vegetarian Gourmet*, *The Fifteen-Minute Single Gourmet* and *Complete Book of Dressings*, survives on the road by changing the order of importance of her meals: "Breakfast becomes number one, because you can usually get healthy breakfast foods at most restaurants: oatmeal, fresh fruit, juice, whole-wheat bread." For lunch Mitchell grabs a low-fat muffin and juice or a sandwich—something light. Dinner is usually broiled fish or chicken with a big salad.

What about vacations—the time when fun takes precedence over following the rules, and diets go out the window?

Nutrition experts recommend indulging—to a point. Treat time can be important on vacations, says Anne Fletcher, M.S., R.D., a nutrition consultant in Minnesota and author of *Thin for Life: Ten Keys to Success from People Who Have Lost Weight and Kept It Off*. As long as you know you're going to go back to your regular diet when you're at home, indulge yourself a bit. This doesn't mean having treats all day long, Fletcher warns, but allowing yourself one to two treats a day when you travel. "In a restaurant, I might enjoy treats like really fine seafood, sorbet, shrimp cocktail, a cappuccino or fresh fruits out of season—foods that are low-fat, that maybe I can't get at home because they're too expensive or my family doesn't like them." Healthy doesn't get put on hold, but you still have the feeling of indulgence.

FLYING HIGH

Everyone has a war story of airline travel: sitting four hours on the tarmac, being stranded in airports far from home, finding nothing remotely edible on the menu. Like a good scout, be prepared when you fly. Bring your own healthy snacks for the plane and enough to tide you over during unexpected layovers: a bagel, boxes of serving-size cereal, bottled water, self-sealing bags of rice cakes, precut fresh vegetables and fruits. "I like to carry dried prunes in individual packets and a low-cal power bar," says Tribole. "It's saved me more than once from those high-fat peanut packs."

It helps to order a special meal before you fly. Get familiar with the airline first, Tribole recommends, since each has different dietary strengths. Some have great seafood meals, others good vegetarian. Call at least 24 hours before flight time and cross your fingers; and, like Jones, plan for emergencies. "I always order a special meal ahead of time," says Jones, "but I have solutions if the meal doesn't show up." Even with standard coach fare, Jones is innovative. On one flight, she scraped the sauce off a chicken breast, chopped the chicken up and put it on the undressed salad. "There was just enough of the sauce that I couldn't completely get off the chicken to dress the salad. I spooned the cooked vegetables from the entrée over the chicken and enjoyed a terrific chicken salad."

Steven Raichlen, a chef and award-winning author of the *High-Flavor, Low-Fat Cooking* series, recommends looking for healthy newcomers in airports before you board. Many airports now have sushi bars, stands that sell nonfat frozen yogurt, fresh fruit stalls or cafés

BEST BETS IN ETHNIC EATING OUT

- **Cajun:** shrimp Creole, seafood jambalaya, boiled shrimp

- **Chinese:** wonton soup, hot-and-sour soup, chicken chow mein, chicken chop suey, vegetable lo mein, Szechwan shrimp, steamed rice, vegetable stir-fries (ask for a "dry stir-fry" made without oil or share a plateful and get double portions of steamed rice), lychee nuts

- **French:** consommé, bouillabaisse (avoid the rouille sauce), salade Niçoise, roast chicken, grilled seafood or chicken, tomato coulis, sorbets, fresh berries

- **Greek:** shish kebab, baked fish, simple rice dishes, yogurt-cucumber sauce, souvlaki, pita bread, plain yogurt with honey

- **Indian:** lentil soups, dal, tandoori chicken, or fish, bean- or grain-based curries, rice pilaf, basmati rice, raita, chapati or naan breads, chutney

- **Italian:** minestrone soup, Italian breads and breadsticks, pasta with marinara sauce, pasta with meatballs, most seafood dishes, chicken cacciatore, Italian sorbets or ices

- **Japanese:** miso soup, grilled fish and lean meats, vegetarian sushi rolls, sukiyaki, teriyaki chicken or vegetables, udon noodles, rice noodles, steamed rice

- **Mexican:** gazpacho soup, salsa, steamed corn tortillas, soft tacos, chicken or beef fajitas (hold the guacamole and sour cream), baked fish, vegetarian chili, mesquite-grilled chicken or fish

- **Middle Eastern:** hummus, tabbouleh, lentil soup, rice

where you can grab a cup of decaf café latte made with skim milk to fill you up between flights.

"If all goes wrong, you can always ask the flight attendant for pretzels," says Melanie Barnard, *Bon Appétit* columnist and author of *Low-Fat Grilling.* Or, as Barnard does, count on room service at your hotel.

ENERGY-BOOSTING FOODS

Dragging through your day? Overscheduled and overworked? How about a quick energy boost? Step right up to an array of healthy foods that will help you breeze through even the most sluggish afternoon. And they're all in your own kitchen—or can be.

A little nutrition know-how goes a long way toward choosing the best energy-boosting foods. Carbohydrates, fat and protein are the three main sources of dietary energy, with carbohydrates being the most important, according to Peter Miller, Ph.D., executive director of the Hilton Head Health Institute in Hilton Head, South Carolina. "Carbohydrates provide an efficient, long-lasting energy source," Dr. Miller says, especially the complex carbs like whole grains, beans, pasta and breads. All give you a more immediate supply of energy to burn. Fats and protein take longer to digest and can slow you down. The trick for consistent energy is "to combine a little protein with a lot of carbohydrate-rich foods," says Somer.

It's also vital to drink lots of water to keep your energy level up, says Somer. Water is essential in the fight against fatigue. A symptom of mild dehydration is fatigue, and often your thirst is not a good indication of your water needs. If you're thirsting for a glass of water, you probably need two.

Avoid dependence on coffee and sugar. They provide quick fixes but little lasting energy. More than three cups of coffee can fuel your fatigue rather than your energy level, says Somer. Sugar-loaded foods cause you to drop even lower when the buzz wears off. Instead of sugar, plan your snacks around nutrient-dense foods that won't deplete essential energy reserves (see page 13).

We're beginning to see more and more how a diet centered on fresh fruits, vegetables, grains and legumes can build these energy reserves. A healthy diet is like a healthy bank account we can draw on in times of stress because it provides important nutrients.

ANTIOXIDANTS

Fresh fruits and vegetables are loaded with antioxidants like vitamin C, vitamin E and beta-carotene. Studies show that antioxidants may help protect our bodies from age-related diseases. Antioxidants are our front-line defense against free radicals, those molecules that damage cells through oxidation, altering the cell's genetic structure and promoting the growth of cancer. Since these nutrients need to be replenished each day, the easiest way to get enough of them is by planning a few servings of fruits and vegetables into every meal.

Fruits or juices can start the day, and you can regularly add vegetable salads to lunch and dinner. An easy way to build vegetables into in-between meals is to always carry carrot and celery sticks in your purse or briefcase.

For a healthy boost of beta-carotene, choose dark-green and sunny-colored vegetables: spinach, leaf lettuce, broccoli, kale, collards, beet greens, winter squash, pumpkin, carrots, sweet potatoes and red, orange and green sweet peppers. Get into the habit of adding half a cupful of one or more beta-rich vegetables to soups, stews and salads, says Dr. Fuchs. Or just serve them steamed or microwaved with a little lemon juice. Another great source of beta-carotene is tropical papaya or mango, delicious as a snack or pureed as an easy dessert topping for low-fat angel food cake or frozen yogurt.

For your daily dose of vitamin C, start your day with a citrus fruit or juice (oranges are tops for nutrient value, says Dr. Fuchs), or add sliced strawberries to morning oatmeal. When you slide up to the salad bar at lunch, scoop up some high-vitamin-C broccoli florets.

As for vitamin E, the richest sources include fortified cereals, sunflower seeds, oils, sweet potatoes and wheat germ. "I put small amounts of wheat germ in everything," says Somer, including the pancake batter for weekend breakfasts.

POWER SNACKING

Snacking has gotten a bad rap, but actually it can be a powerful source of sustained energy. Here's the way it works: If you're eating healthy snacks, snacking is healthy. See the box on page 13 for quick ideas.

Plan a few of these healthy snacks into each day, suggests Fletcher. Don't leave snacking to chance or wait until you're hungry to decide —because you'll usually grab the doughnuts sitting out in the coffee room, a bag of salty chips from the vending machine or the box of cookies you have stashed in the cupboard. When Fletcher surveyed people who'd lost weight and kept it off, she found that most of them planned snacks into their daily eating. "My rule is: If I'm hungry after several hours and it's not time for lunch, it's time for a snack. So I try to have something on hand," says Fletcher. "It's long periods without eating that lead to bingeing and overeating." Think healthy, and it becomes a habit, says Asanovic. It takes no longer to pack fruit at home than to walk to a vending machine at work.

But for those last-minute stops at vending machines and convenience stores, here's a quick list of the best low-fat snacks we found:

- Barbara's Bakery Fat-Free Organic Sourdough Pretzels
- Barbara's Bakery Organic Whole Wheat Pretzels
- Guiltless Gourmet Baked Not Fried Tortilla Chips
- Frito-Lay Low Fat Baked Tostitos
- Baked Lay's Low Fat Original Potato Chips
- Fit Foods Original Flavor Low Fat Baked Potato Chips
- Mr. Phipps Tater Crisps
- Bugles Light
- Health Valley 100% Natural Fruit Bar
- Health Valley Fat-Free Granola Bar
- Fat-Free Snackwells Cereal Bars
- Keebler Reduced-Fat Pecan Sandies
- R.W. Frookie Oatmeal Raisin Fat-Free Cookie
- Entenmann's Fat-Free Oatmeal Raisin Cookies
- Häagen-Dazs Fat-Free Sorbet 'N Yogurt Bars

BROWN BAG BONUSES

Packing your own lunch has its advantages: You can be sure just how many calories and fat grams go into your midday meal, and you can have something tasty to look forward to all morning—as long as you avoid brown bag boredom.

To get beyond the peanut-butter-and-jelly syndrome, experts say, use leftovers. Well-planned leftovers lead to luscious lunches. So when you prepare dinner or cook ahead on the weekend, think quantity. Cook double, then pack away portions in serving-size microwaveable containers. You'll have a superstar selection of homemade lunches, ready to grab and go. Just reheat them in your office microwave.

Our experts all had their favorites: leftover meat loaf or baked chicken served cold or sliced into sandwiches; extra stir-fried vegetables tossed with low-fat dressing (by lunch they'll have marinated into an Italian antipasto, great with a crusty whole-grain roll); leftover cooked pasta topped with steamed broccoli, kidney beans and a bit of Parmesan cheese; baked potato halves smothered with steamed

20 Favorite Quick and Healthy Snacks

1. Low-fat trail mix: low-fat miniature pretzels, oyster crackers, low-fat wheat thins, low-fat cheese crackers

2. Frozen unsweetened raspberries, cherries, bananas

3. Fresh whole fruit like apples, oranges, bananas, peaches and plums

4. Precut carrots, celery, jicama and other salad bar vegetables

5. Low-fat, low-sugar cereals in individual cartons

6. Dried prunes or raisins in individual packets

7. Fruit sorbets or ices (higher vitamin C and often less fat than frozen yogurt)

8. Low-fat, low-sodium instant soups

9. Baked sweet potatoes drizzled with low-sodium soy sauce

10. Baked potatoes with melted low-fat cheese

11. Rice cakes or caramel-flavored popcorn cakes

12. Raita (an Indian spread of nonfat plain yogurt, fresh mint and chopped cucumber) on whole-grain crackers or bread

13. Baked tortilla chips and salsa

14. Pita pizzas with low-fat cheese

15. Nonfat vanilla frozen yogurt in half a cantaloupe

16. Sugar-free root beer with low-fat or fat-free ice cream or frozen yogurt

17. Whole cherry tomatoes

18. Whole-wheat pretzels

19. Fat-free crackers topped with low-fat cheese

20. Air-popped popcorn

Top Chain Choices

Food	Fat (g.)	Calories
Arby's		
Light Roast Chicken Deluxe	6	276
Light Roast Turkey Deluxe	7	260
Junior Roast Beef	14	324
Burger King		
BK Broiler Chicken Sandwich	6	550
Plain hamburger	15	330
Broiled chicken salad without dressing	4	200
Garden Salad with 2 tablespoons reduced-calorie Italian dressing	3.5	115
Hardee's		
Grilled Chicken Sandwich	9	290
Regular Roast Beef	11	270
Grilled Chicken Salad	3	150
Pancakes, plain (3)	2	280
Kentucky Fried Chicken		
Tender Roast Chicken breast without skin	4.3	169
Tender Roast Chicken thigh without skin	5.5	106

vegetables and melted low-fat cheese. On chilly days, expand your repertoire to bean or grain soups or stews.

Add minitreats—a couple of low-fat fig newtons, cut-up fresh fruit or a container of low-fat yogurt. You may not need the additional food at lunch, but you'll welcome it at three o'clock.

FAST FOODS

Fast food is a way of life; even the nutritional experts we interviewed went to Burger King or McDonald's when life got especially hectic. Luckily, today's fast food is not always fat food and healthy meals are available at most drive-throughs—you just have to know what to ask for.

Food	Fat (g.)	Calories
McDonald's		
McLean Deluxe	12	350
McGrilled Chicken Classic	4	260
Fajita Chicken Salad	6	160
Side Salad with 1 package Lite Vinaigrette dressing	4	95
Subway		
Turkey Breast Sub	4	276
Ham Sub	4	273
Roast Beef Sub	6	299
Veggie Delite Sub (all subs with onions, lettuce, tomatoes, pickles, green peppers and olives only)	3	223
Taco Bell		
Light Chicken Soft Taco	5	180
Light Chicken Burrito	6	290
Light Chicken Burrito Supreme	10	410
Wendy's		
Grilled Chicken Fillet Sandwich	7	290
Junior hamburger	10	270
Plain baked potato	0	310
Large chili	10	310

Elizabeth Somer might decide to swing by a fast-food chain on the way home at night, but she always asks for all the meals to be prepared without sauce and orders orange juice instead of soda. When she gets the meals home, she supplements them with fresh fruit and vegetable slices. "Then the total fat content of the fast food meal has been diluted with all kinds of healthy choices," says Somer, so it fits into a healthy dinner.

Pat Baird, R.D., a nutrition consultant and author of *The Pyramid Cookbook*, pops in to McDonald's for grilled chicken and low-fat milk, or a fajita chicken salad and low-fat frozen yogurt. If you choose carefully, the occasional fast-food meal can be part of a healthy lifestyle.

Just don't make fast foods a daily habit. "Even with lower-fat choices, you get fewer fruits and vegetables and less variety than with at-home meals," says Baird. Most fast food items are high in fat and calories, and most people in the drive-through lane opt for the highest-calorie choices: burger, fries and milkshake. A meal of these three could contain your entire daily quota of calories and fat, and half the sodium.

If fast food is part of your weekly meal plan, become familiar with the lower-fat items on your favorite chain's menu. You can even ask at the counter for nutritional information. Read through it and note which of your favorite items are lowest in fat and calories.

Mainly, when ordering in the fast lane, forget the fried foods. Anything breaded or crispy is probably laden with fat. And avoid meals with the words *cheese*, *triple* or *supreme* in the title, Somer says. These automatically add extra calories and fat. Best bet? Grilled chicken sandwich without sauce. Grilled is leaner, and you'll get more flavor for your fat grams.

It helps to decide what you want before you arrive. Our chart of top choices for fast-food dining can get you started.

LETTUCE DANCE

*B*ypass the burgers and waltz up to the salad bar for a great way to eat fast and low-fat on rushed lunch hours. To get less fat than that burger would give you, experts recommend:

• A baked potato topped with salad-bar veggies and lemon juice, plus a tablespoon of grated Parmesan cheese

• An antipasto salad of sliced lean turkey breast over green peppers, cauliflower, mushrooms, onions and tomatoes, topped with beans and low-fat Italian dressing

• A lean Cobb salad of chopped romaine, shredded cabbage, broccoli, shredded carrots, shredded beets and three-bean salad with a drizzle of low-fat blue cheese dressing

• Tuna salad mixed with lots of shredded carrots and packed into a whole-wheat roll

• Spinach leaves with chopped egg, shredded carrots, alfalfa sprouts, mushrooms, broccoli and lean sliced turkey breast, with lemon juice and a little grated Parmesan cheese

CHAPTER 2

TIMESAVING
TIPS AND
LOW-FAT
TECHNIQUES

IN AND OUT OF THE KITCHEN

What's the easiest way to save time in the kitchen? Plan ahead. Cooking quick and healthy on the home front isn't an accident. Most experts recommend that you set aside weekly planning time—as little as 10 minutes on Saturday morning will do—to think about what you'll need for that week. Otherwise, kitchen time equals frustration, pure and simple.

Avoid trying to solve the problem of how to fix a healthy meal 30 minutes before you have to set it on the table. That makes it too easy to run out for takeout chicken (again). Instead, if you've planned for the rush, you can open your refrigerator to an amazing array of healthy ingredients and the makings of a great dinner.

Part of your plan is learning to shop smarter and stocking up on healthy ingredients that take only 5 to 15 minutes to fix. Experts say your weekly shopping trip can be trimmed to 20 minutes once a week with practice and this kind of planning. You'll need a little time up front to educate yourself on favorite choices from the varieties of healthy convenience foods that line the supermarket shelves these days. But shopping for and stocking a good selection of these in your kitchen is the first key to making actual meal preparation a snap.

In addition, learn how to make cooking more fun by enlisting help from kids and other family members. If meals are simple, kids love to help, and traditionally time-consuming jobs go faster.

What we eat—and how we approach eating—clearly has an impact on our health and energy. By approaching weeknight meals with planning, smart shopping and the quick-cooking recipes in this book, you'll make cooking dinner a relaxing and enjoyable part of your day.

MAKING A PLAN

It may seem daunting to think of sitting down on Sunday and planning what you'll be eating for the rest of the week. But here are the advantages: only one trip to the supermarket instead of three or four, buying fewer impulse items, and eating more balanced meals with more variety. If you're new to this, try planning three meals the first week, says author Evelyn Tribole, M.S., R.D., a nutritionist in private practice in Beverly Hills, California, and author of *Healthy Homestyle Cooking*. Choose three favorite dinner menus you can double to provide great lunch leftovers. And if you can, cook certain staples like rice ahead of time.

To make it even easier, build your shopping list throughout the week, says Paulette Mitchell, a cooking instructor and consultant in Minneapolis, Minnesota, and author of *The Fifteen-Minute Vegetarian Gourmet*, *The Fifteen-Minute Single Gourmet* and *Complete Book of Dressings*. She tapes a blank sheet of paper inside her pantry cabinet door and writes down staples she needs as she runs out. This makes it easy to plan on the weekend what her family will be eating for the week. "I revolve our dinners around a few favorite meals, then I try to serve leftovers in slightly different forms the rest of the week," says Mitchell. Plus she builds in a reserve of one-dish meals, such as a big pot of soup, for really rushed evenings.

Keep your meal plans super simple to start. Don't try to orchestrate a symphony when preparing dinner after a busy day; choose two or three dishes that are fast and filling and that leave you with great leftovers. Follow the easy menu plans in this book. Each focuses on one main dish, like Pinto Bean Chili (page 32), then offers accompaniments that can be made while the main dish cooks, like Jalapeño-Buttermilk Cornbread (page 31). The game plan for each menu lets you know what to cook first to streamline dinner preparation. "The meals that succeed in our house are meals that are fast and simple," says author Elizabeth Somer, R.D., author of *Food and Mood*. "Forget the gourmet, focus on healthy." That's what you'll be doing. And that doesn't mean sacrificing flavor, as you'll see when you try the delicious recipes in this book.

As you plan, be sure to include variety—but also repeat family favorites like meat loaf or stew. Familiar good-tasting foods on the menu each night make healthy eating easier for most people, says Tribole.

"You have to view healthy cooking and shopping as a project, and for any project, a plan is essential," says Michele Tuttle, M.P.H., R.D., director of consumer affairs at the Food Marketing Institute in Washington D.C. Lots of people are very resistant to planning meals, but it saves time, food and energy—and makes shopping much easier. "Even if you just plan the big meals like dinner," says Tuttle, "it allows you to think about your week and take into account scheduling constraints, guests and nights out."

SUPERMARKET SAVVY

You're standing in the supermarket line, watching the woman ahead of you pile her groceries onto the checkout counter. Silently you evaluate your choices and compare. Once again, you've picked up that bag of chocolate chip cookies and a few cartons of ice cream—they looked good, you forgot your list and you were hungry (real hungry, judging by the opened cookie bag). Shopping isn't your favorite thing, anyway.

A good shopping strategy would have gotten you home with better choices. Being smart in the supermarket is crucial—next in importance after good planning—for healthy weeknight meals. Read the hints from leading nutritionists and chefs that follow—and see how they learned to make wise choices that don't foil good eating intentions.

1. Use Your List. The experts agree: Without a list, shopping takes longer. You'll be less focused, says Tribole, and more likely to be seduced by impulse buys.

With practice, you can create your week's menus and shopping list in less than ten minutes. You can still be flexible and watch for sales: If lean ground beef is half price, you can switch from chicken to meat loaf and buy extra to freeze for next week's spaghetti and meatballs.

Several kitchen experts had a neat device that makes shopping fast and fun: a diagram of their grocery store. Most stores have these, or you can make your own. Run off multiple copies and use them as shopping lists, says Steven Raichlen, a chef and award-winning author of the *High-Flavor, Low-Fat Cooking* series. Raichlen groups items by where they are located in the store: dairy is first, then paper products, dry goods, produce. When we tested this theory, we got in and out of the store in no time flat.

2. Shop the Same Store. In unfamiliar markets, you waste valuable time going down aisle after aisle, hunting for your favorite foods, says Somer. "I've gotten to the point where I know exactly what I want in my store and I can pick it up without even looking at it." If you use a list to cluster your items in certain aisles, says Tuttle, you can go through each aisle only once and get your groceries fast.

"Even if another store is having a sale, I stick with my favorite store," says Colleen Miner, author of *Together in the Kitchen* and a chef on a weekly Minneapolis television show. "If I want to shop quickly, I go where I know where everything is."

Every once in a while, Miner suggests, spend a few minutes looking at new products you might like to try. New convenience products come out every month that can make it easy for you to maintain a healthy lifestyle. If you don't see what you want, be sure to ask the store manager to stock it.

3. Shop the Slow Times. When you shop is as important as how you shop. Choosing the right time can save you the extra ten minutes of waiting in long checkout lines. If you go right after work, you'll join hundreds of other hungry, frazzled shoppers during the typical supermarket's rush hour. Also avoid Saturdays, the worst day to shop. Best time? Later in the evening around seven or eight o'clock, says Tuttle, when most people are eating dinner.

If you're an early riser with jam-packed evenings, stop in before work. This worked for several of our experts, who even had time to unpack and store groceries at home before starting off to work.

4. Increase Your Label IQ. Part of educating yourself to make quick and nutritious meals is understanding and reading food nutrient labels. First pay attention to serving size, says Tribole. If you don't, the rest of the information on the label is meaningless. "Ask yourself what your realistic serving size for this food is. If the label on the can of soup says two servings but you usually heat up the whole can for lunch, you have to multiply all the nutrients by two," she says.

Then look at what that amount gives you as a percentage of your recommended daily allowance of fat, sodium and calories.

If the product you're buying has 60 percent of a day's worth of sodium, you know that when you add it to the rest of your meals that day it will shoot you way past your limit. "So ask yourself if it's worth it to you taste-wise and flavor-wise," says Tribole. There are no forbidden foods, she stresses, just the need to be aware of what you're eating and try to achieve a balanced diet in the long run. "As a general rule, I advise people to aim for no more than 5 grams of fat and no more than 300 milligrams of sodium per serving," says Anita Hirsch, M.S., R.D., nutritionist at Rodale Press and staff nutritionist for *Quick and Healthy Cooking* magazine.

Here are basic steps to increase your label reading IQ without enrolling in a nutrition course:

■ Look at the first few ingredients—they are ranked in order of quantity.

■ Check the portion or serving size.

■ Check the amount of calories, fat and sodium for each portion. Is it within your daily amount?

■ Watch for excess sugar in disguise ("Words ending in *-ose* mean sugar," warns Nan Kathryn Fuchs, Ph.D., a nutritionist in private practice in Sebastopol, California, nutrition editor of *Women's Health Letter* and author of *Overcoming the Legacy of Overeating*.).

■ Check "percentage of daily value" of important nutrients like calcium, vitamins A and C and iron. Reread labels occasionally, even with your favorite foods, advises Tribole. You'd be surprised how often they change.

5. Bulk Up. Shop in bulk, suggests author Anne Fletcher, M.S., R.D., a nutrition consultant in Minnesota and author of *Thin for Life: Ten Keys to Success from People Who Have Lost Weight and Kept It Off*. Most experts we interviewed buy big bags of frozen vegetables and frozen boneless, skinless chicken breasts to have on hand for speedy meals.

Stock up on staples you use regularly. Say you eat pasta three times a week. Buy a lot at once—even a one- or two-month supply, says Tuttle. "Get in the habit of thinking a week in advance or even longer," she says. "Why not have a few extra loaves of bread in the freezer, a few extra boxes of cereal if you have room in your pantry?" Stocking up means fewer trips to the store—you only shop when you need to replenish perishable items.

For extra convenience, supplement your shopping trips with delivery service. Chef Raichlen makes use of free local delivery services from markets he shops regularly. Call fish markets, bakeries, smaller grocery stores and dairy delivery companies—you may find home delivery a real bargain and a way to cut your shopping time in half.

6. Mind Your P's: Perimeter and Produce. Two important guidelines once you're in the store: Stick to the outer perimeter where the basics are, and focus most of your shopping time in the produce section.

"Most fresh foods are located along the perimeter walls where plumbing and electrical fixtures are housed," says Tribole. Packaged nonperishables usually line the center aisles. Fill up your cart with perimeter shopping first and you'll be less likely to browse in the tempting center of the store.

Secondly, try to spend most of your time in the produce aisle, since fresh fruits and vegetables form the foundation of most of the healthy recipes in this book. It's also a major resource for great snack foods, says Somer. "Look for precut vegetables and fresh snacking fruit— bananas, oranges, kiwis." And don't forget those cruciferous vegetables. Hirsch recommends buying a different cruciferous vegetable each time you shop—broccoli one week, cauliflower the next—so they're always part of your meals.

7. Eat First. Don't shop when you're hungry, warns Tuttle—a growling tummy can tempt you to grab less nutritious snacks like doughnuts or an extra bag of trail mix from the bulk bins. Plan to have a piece of fruit or a glass of juice before you leave for the store.

8. Collect Convenience. Look for foods that are healthy but also cook fast: instant brown rice, precut produce. "I buy foods that don't require a lot of preparation," says Marie Simmons, *Bon Appétit* columnist and author of *Fresh & Fast: Inspired Cooking for Every Season & Every Day*. Simmons loads her shopping cart with cored and peeled pineapple, red potatoes that don't have to be peeled and spinach in bags. "Fresh is the key, good taste is the key." Make it easy on yourself.

COOK IN QUANTITY

Every expert we talked with follows another important rule: Cook favorite dishes in quantity. Why waste time making rice twice, when you can cook up a big pot that'll last all week?

Dr. Fuchs recommends having containers of cooked whole grains— brown rice, millet, pasta—frozen in one-, two- or four-serving portions. They're great for five-minute dinners; you can reheat these smaller portions in two to four minutes in the microwave. "It's also useful if you're cooking for different taste buds in one family—you

Quickest-Cooking Meats, Seafood and Poultry

Beef

Extra-lean ground
beef
Flank steak
Stew meat

Poultry

Boneless skinless
chicken breasts
Boneless skinless
turkey breasts
Turkey tenderloin
Ground chicken or
turkey

Pork

Boneless loin
chops
Lean ham

Lamb

Loin chops
Stew meat

Seafood

Fish fillets
Scallops
Shrimp
Crabmeat
Clams
Mussels

like brown rice, your husband likes white," says Dr. Fuchs. "You can have a supply of both in the freezer, and it takes no time to reheat them."

"I routinely cook up batches of favorite soups to freeze," says nutrition consultant and author Patricia Baird, R.D. With homemade stock, experts recommend using a fat separator or chilling the soup to allow fat to rise to the top where it can be skimmed off. Soups are best frozen flat on a tray in resealable plastic freezer bags, then stacked. A big pot of vegetable-laden soup starts the week's nutrition off right. "Use vegetables like carrots and winter squash," says Dr. Fuchs. "For extra nutrition put in white beans, rice, barley or millet. For energy, potatoes or yams. When you're reheating the soup, throw in nutritious chopped greens such as spinach or chard."

Experts also suggest asking yourself, What can I do today that will make tomorrow's dinner easier? Doubling up on tasks—like chopping onions—cuts kitchen time in half. Do quantity cooking while you're working around the house, reading, or catching up on chores. "Whenever I am home," says Susan G. Purdy, author of *Have Your Cake and Eat It, Too* and *Let Them Eat Cake*, "something is simmering on the stove or baking in the oven." A soup, casserole or thick hearty stew for the week's meals can cook without too much supervision while you do other things. Just set a kitchen timer to remind you.

Save money by cooking large batches of your own convenience

foods. Susan Asanovic, M.S., R.D., owner of the food and nutrition consulting firm Table Dans Le Bon Sens in Wilton, Connecticut, cooks a huge pot of beans regularly and freezes them. Fletcher's family loves baked potatoes, so she always cooks extra for lunches during the week; topped with vegetables and melted low-fat cheese, they're a favorite 5-minute meal.

Stocking your fridge and freezer with this kind of planned quantity cooking will make you feel rich in time. You'll always have the makings of a wealth of nutritious meals.

PLAN ON THE WEEKEND

Planned-overs, says Tribole, are intentional leftovers, a most important strategy for healthy weeknight meals. A 30-minute cooking session on the weekend gives you a two- or three-meal head start for the week. Look over your menus for the week. If you're having rice twice and macaroni in three meals, cook up a big pot of each on Sunday. Drain well, rinse in cold water to remove excess starch (and keep the stickiness down) and let the rice or pasta cool. Then package in flattened resealable plastic storage bags or small containers.

Spanish rice or macaroni and cheese is super-easy when the grain is already cooked—all you have to do is assemble and bake. A pot of cooked rice can also become the base for an impromptu stir-fry, a quick tomato-rice soup or a salad with low-fat vinaigrette and leftover steamed vegetables. Chef Raichlen uses up leftover cooked beans by adding sautéed onions, garlic and cumin. It's a natural way of thinking for food experts: What can I make ahead to make cooking a breeze?

Include certain perishable staples in your cook-ahead session each week to save actual prep time on busy nights. If you're chopping an onion in the food processor, why not chop two? Busy cooks often have bags of chopped onions in the freezer—they don't freeze solid, so you can scoop out a cup or tablespoon when you need it. Treat other repeat ingredients the same way: a week's worth of minced fresh garlic, chopped fresh parsley and homemade low-fat pesto in the refrigerator are worth their weight in gold on weeknights.

Marinating firm cuts of fish or chicken in self-sealing plastic bags is another popular prep-ahead tactic chefs use to reduce kitchen time. Simply place the cleaned meat in a freezer-weight bag and add lime or lemon juice, a little olive oil, tomato juice, citrus peel, low-fat plain yogurt, curry—whatever appeals to your taste buds. The tanginess of the yogurt or citrus helps reduce the need for salt, and your meat will tenderize as it marinates. Refrigerate the bag for up to two days, turning it occasionally to distribute the marinade evenly. Raichlen depends on low-fat marinades like these to transform lean ingredients into memorable dishes. He keeps a variety of quick marinades on hand during the week (favorites are a Cuban combination of lime juice, minced garlic and ground cumin and an Indian mixture of nonfat plain yogurt, lemon juice, minced onion and saffron).

Once you try this trick for boosting flavor, your summer menus will revolve around the grill, as Raichlen's do. "You can also reduce the marinade as a low-fat sauce," he suggests. Just boil at high heat for 3 to 5 minutes, then drizzle over the cooked meat.

Raichlen also makes yogurt cheese each week. It's a simple overnight procedure: Spoon a container of nonfat plain yogurt into a strainer lined with cheesecloth, place over a bowl and refrigerate overnight. In the morning you have a thick, creamy fat-free base for favorite desserts, dips and sauces. Raichlen uses yogurt cheese for his signature whipped pudding of yogurt cheese, vanilla, lemon peel and a little sugar, and for his winning tart filling that he tops with fresh fruit.

Here are some favorite prep-ahead items we found in our experts' refrigerators and freezers:

- Lemon juice (juice 10 lemons and freeze in ice-cube trays)
- Minced onions (mince 3 to 5 onions in your food processor and freeze in ½-cup portions)
- Minced garlic (mince 2 to 3 whole heads of garlic and store covered with olive oil or lemon juice in the fridge)
- Bread crumbs (place stale bread in a food processor, grind and freeze for breading foods and topping casseroles)
- Cooked beans (soak and cook triple batches, then freeze in resealable plastic bags)
- Cooked brown, white and basmati rice (freeze in 1-cup portions)
- Chopped ginger (chop in the food processor—don't bother to peel it—and freeze in 1-tablespoon portions in ice-cube trays)

ENLIST YOUR FAMILY'S HELP

Even with careful planning and a stockpile of leftovers, you still have to assemble the meal. How do the experts get weeknight dinners from stove to table—and have fun doing it?

"Delegate," says Asanovic. "Enlist family members to help shop, prep and clean up. We all have just 24 hours in a day. Healthy, delicious food is a huge priority, but I don't like drudgery. So I organize, prioritize and stay focused."

Children should be engaged in helping in the kitchen, agrees Simmons. "It's an act of love; you're nurturing and sustaining them as you cook together. Part of health is family time. Give each child a task: setting the table, slicing the bread." And watch dinner appear like magic!

TOP TOOLS FOR THE SPEEDY KITCHEN

When we asked our experts for their favorite timesaving tools, here's what they recommended.

Food Processor. Nothing beats a food processor for cutting vegetables, pureeing, or grating cheese in literally seconds. Raichlen uses it to make instant sauces or sorbets out of frozen berries. You can mince your fresh herbs, onions and garlic in minutes or puree part of a soup to thicken the whole pot.

Keep your food processor plugged in and on the counter, say the experts, so you'll use it often. With lower-fat cooking, there's less cleanup too. Just rinse the work bowl and blade between different uses in the same meal.

Wok. Asian chefs can put a fast delicious dinner on the table because they wok it. Stir-fries cooked quickly at high heat in a wok also retain maximum nutrients, color and flavor for minimum fat. The best woks are carbon steel—the favorite of many chefs because it distributes heat evenly. Follow the manufacturer's directions for seasoning your wok before you use it—only once is needed.

To save time when wokking, keep the heat high. Have ingredients cut and sauces ready, since cooking time can be less than five minutes for a vegetable stir-fry for four people.

Pressure Cooker. Pressure cookers have evolved big time since the days of Grandma's spaghetti sauce on the ceiling. If you want to add the superior nutrition of whole grains to your meals on a regular basis, invest in a pressure cooker. The new models are shiny and efficient, with complex safety backup systems—foolproof and fast.

Most whole grains, longer-cooking vegetables, soups and pasta sauces can be pressure-cooked in half the time. You simply put the food inside, lock on the lid, set the pressure cooker over high heat and let the steam pressure build. The boiling point rises from 212°—the highest you can get in a regular pot—to 250°. It is the best way to maximize nutrients: The food is done sooner and the nutrient-filled steam goes back into the pot.

Experts advise filling the pressure cooker only half to three-quarters full, to allow the steam pressure enough room to build. When high pressure is reached, begin timing. Newer pressure cookers have an indicator on the lid that tells you when they reach high pressure.

Best buys are stainless steel, a solid bottom of copper or aluminum (for best heat conduction) and a six-quart capacity.

Sizzle Plate. A terrific restaurant tool rarely used in home kitchens is making news: the sizzle plate. It's a concave metal dish with a wide rim. You arrange meat, fish, poultry and vegetables in the center, add a drizzle of liquid such as defatted stock or juice, cover it with foil and pop it into the oven. Minutes later, you have a meal. Because it works on the principle of moist-heat cooking, many of the nutrients are retained. Sizzle plates are available in most kitchenware stores. Look for 10″ × 7″ plates in stainless steel for the most versatility.

Microwave. When was the last time you actually *cooked* in your microwave (not just reheated something)? This timesaving device can speed meal preparation dramatically. You can make breakfast in 2 minutes, lunch in 5, dinner in 15 if you depend on microwave magic.

You don't have to gussy up food with oil or butter to keep it moist when you microwave. Just cover it with plastic wrap and vent. The moist heat cooking can produce incredibly low-fat meals. And nutritionists love the microwave because fewer vitamins are lost than in most other cooking methods. "Microwaving retains nutrients best," says Asanovic. Cornell University food scientists found that microwaving lost the least vitamin C in broccoli, compared to boiling and steaming. And you lose more fat, according to a study at Texas A&M University, which looked at the amount of fat from ground beef zapped by microwaves as opposed to other cooking methods.

And there's a bonus for especially busy nights: If you use the microwave for quickly cooked fresh vegetables, there are no pots to clean, dry and put away.

SPEEDY STOVETOP AND OVEN TIPS

Use these four cooking methods for the quickest, healthiest meals.

Grilling. Both outdoor gas and indoor stovetop grilling are speedy ways of retaining flavor and moistness as you cook leaner cuts of meats and fish. Try marinating vegetables and meat overnight in self-sealing plastic bags in the refrigerator. Brush foods with a basting liquid while grilling (try balsamic vinegar or low-fat chicken stock) to further prevent drying out. Cut cleanup by grilling on heavy-duty foil. (Avoid charcoal grills, which take 30 minutes to heat up.)

Broiling. Broiling takes 5 to 10 minutes for most meats and fish and is best for those thinner cuts that tend to dry out or stick on the grill. Coat broiler pans or racks with no-stick cooking spray or line them with foil. Baste leaner meats and chicken fillets with balsamic vinegar, pineapple juice, lemon juice or chicken broth during broiling to enhance their flavor.

Stir-Frying. Usually done in a wok or large skillet where there's room to toss the food, stir-frying is the fastest way to cook most vegetables, as well as boneless chicken and shrimp. This method is preferred by Asian chefs because the high-heat, quick cooking retains much of the original color and texture of vegetables.

Steam-Sautéing (Quick Braising). Braising, or slow cooking in flavored liquids, tenderizes leaner cuts of meat. You can speed up the process with a quick, high-heat sauté to sear meat in a tiny amount of oil or chicken broth. Then add more broth or other flavorful liquid, cover and steam until tender.

KITCHEN SHORTCUTS

■ Have all the ingredients and equipment out before you begin to cook.

■ Use no-stick cookware to avoid oiling the pan.

■ Keep your food processor and blender on the counter for quick access.

■ Chop and shred vegetables in your food processor.

■ Prepare two or more recipes at the same time.

■ Keep your work area clear by cleaning up as you go: replace jar lids, package leftover vegetables, put used bowls and spoons in the dishwasher.

FRESHNESS IN THE FRIDGE

■ Store foods in the fridge by types: produce in crisper drawers, beverages in the side door where they can't ice up, fresh foods toward the front where you'll see and use them quickly.

■ Store uncooked meats, fish and poultry in the coldest part of your fridge.

■ Store leftovers in see-through containers.

■ Store washed, torn lettuce in your salad spinner. The small amount of water left in the bottom under the spinner basket will humidify greens and keep them crisp for 5 to 7 days.

■ Store fresh herbs standing in a glass of water loosely covered with a plastic bag. Or wrap a moist paper towel around the stems and store them in perforated resealable plastic vegetable bags.

■ Store mushrooms and strawberries unwashed in a paper bag or cardboard carton (not the crisper drawer), loosely covered with paper towels to absorb excess water.

Meals in Minutes
with Your Microwave

Best Breakfasts

- **Egg and Cheese Sandwich:** Make your own egg-and-cheese sandwich. Break an egg into a microwaveable custard cup, beat with a small amount of water and microwave at half power (50%) for 1 minute, or until the egg is cooked. Layer it on a toasted English muffin with a slice of low-fat cheese.

- **Breakfast Pizza:** If you love leftover pizza for breakfast, make your own in a flash. Top a halved English muffin with leftover spaghetti sauce and shredded low-fat cheese and place on a paper towel. Microwave on high power for 1 to 2 minutes, or until the cheese melts.

Lightning Lunches

- **Baked Stuffed Potato:** Bake a scrubbed potato by pricking it with a fork and microwaving on high power for 4 to 5 minutes; slit open. Top with frozen or precooked vegetables and shredded low-fat cheese. Microwave for 1 minute longer.

- **Pasta Presto:** Add 1 cup mixed frozen vegetables to 1 cup cooked leftover pasta. Top with 1 tablespoon each lemon juice and grated Parmesan cheese and cover with plastic wrap. Microwave on high power for 2 minutes.

Desperation Dinners

- **Quick Tomato Sauce:** Create a fast tomato sauce by combining 4 cups chopped tomatoes, 2 tablespoons minced garlic and 3 tablespoons minced fresh basil; cover and microwave on high power for 5 minutes, then puree. Toss with pasta.

- **Fast Fish:** Wrap a fish fillet and salad bar vegetables in parchment. Microwave on high power for 4 to 5 minutes, or until the fish flakes when pressed lightly with a fork. Sprinkle the fish with lemon juice.

CHAPTER 3

SIMPLE
COMFORT
IN ONE POT

$\mathcal{S}$PEEDY SOUP AND STEW DINNERS

$\mathcal{A}$ big pot of soul-warming soup always tastes as if it's been simmering on low for hours, lovingly tended by a culinary wizard (like Grandma). But most of these savory one-pot dinners are ready in 30 minutes. And leftovers taste even better the next day, when seasonings mellow. Our collection of rush-hour soups and hearty stews will make old-fashioned flavor and good nutrition an easy part of your weeknight menus.

SPEEDY SOUTHWESTERN DINNER

Pinto Bean Chili
Jalapeño Buttermilk Cornbread
Tossed Green Salad

*C*hili and cornbread can fit into busy weeknights if you cook smart. Use canned pinto beans and precut vegetables from the salad bar, and bake the cornbread while the chili simmers. Then thicken the chili with a quick puree instead of lengthy cooking time.

GAME PLAN

1. Prepare the cornbread and put it in the oven to bake.
2. Start the chili.
3. Make a tossed salad from mixed baby lettuces, shredded carrots and diced tomatoes. Add your favorite low-fat dressing.

JALAPEÑO BUTTERMILK CORNBREAD

SERVES 6

1½	cups yellow or white cornmeal
½	cup all-purpose flour
2	teaspoons baking powder
½	teaspoon baking soda
½	teaspoon salt
1	tablespoon oil
1	tablespoon honey
2	eggs, slightly beaten
1½	cups low-fat buttermilk
⅓	cup frozen whole-kernel corn, thawed and drained
3–4	tablespoons chopped jalapeño peppers (wear plastic gloves when handling)

Coat an 8″ × 8″ baking pan or a 9″ ovenproof skillet with no-stick cooking spray and place it in the oven. Turn the oven to 450° and heat the pan for 3 to 5 minutes, or until it is very hot.

While the pan is heating, in a medium bowl combine the cornmeal, flour, baking powder, baking soda, salt, oil, honey, eggs, buttermilk, corn and jalapeño peppers. Beat vigorously for 30 seconds. Pour into the hot pan.

Reduce the oven to 375° and bake for 20 minutes, or until the cornbread is golden brown and a toothpick inserted in the center comes out clean. Let the cornbread cool slightly, then cut it into 6 pieces.

Preparation time: 6 minutes
Cooking time: 20 minutes

Chef's note: Leftover cornbread can be stored in the refrigerator for up to 3 days if it's wrapped tightly in plastic wrap. Toast thin slices of cornbread and spread them with jam for a quick breakfast.

Per serving: 239 calories, 5.7 g. fat (21% of calories), 5.2 g. dietary fiber, 73 mg. cholesterol, 551 mg. sodium.

PINTO BEAN CHILI

SERVES 4

1   *cup defatted reduced-sodium chicken broth*

2   *cups chopped onions*

½   *cup chopped celery*

½   *cup shredded carrots*

2–3   *tablespoons minced garlic*

2   *teaspoons ground cumin*

4   *teaspoons chili powder*

1   *can (16 ounces) reduced-sodium pinto beans, undrained*

1   *can (16 ounces) reduced-sodium low-fat barbecue baked beans*

2   *teaspoons chopped jalapeño peppers (wear plastic gloves when handling)*

1   *can (16 ounces) reduced-sodium chopped Italian plum tomatoes (with juice)*

  Salt and ground black pepper

⅓   *cup shredded low-fat Monterey Jack cheese*

½   *cup nonfat sour cream*

In a large Dutch oven over medium-high heat, bring ½ cup of the broth to a boil. Add the onions; cook and stir for 2 minutes. Add the celery, carrots, garlic, cumin and chili powder; cook and stir for 3 minutes.

Add the pinto beans, baked beans, jalapeño peppers, tomatoes (with juice) and remaining ½ cup of the broth. Increase the heat to high; cover the pot and bring the chili to a boil. Reduce the heat to medium high; simmer the chili, covered, for 15 minutes, stirring occasionally. (Adjust the heat so that the chili is cooking rapidly but not scorching.)

To thicken the chili, place 4 cups in a blender or food processor and carefully puree it on low speed. Return the pureed chili to the pot; add salt and pepper to taste. If desired, add more chili powder and chopped jalapeño peppers to taste.

Spoon the chili into 4 bowls; stir in the Monterey Jack. Top each bowl with a dollop of sour cream.

Preparation time: 10 minutes
Cooking time: 25 minutes

Per serving: 325 calories, 4.1 g. fat (10% of calories), 11.1 g. dietary fiber, 7 mg. cholesterol, 717 mg. sodium.

BEEF IT UP!

Savory Beef Stew
Chive Biscuits
Carrot Raisin Salad

*P*ressure cooking gives this speedy stew slow-cooked flavor. And the drop biscuits cook in minutes. To keep the biscuits lean yet tender, we replaced some of the butter with yogurt and low-fat buttermilk. If you don't have a pressure cooker, follow the directions for using a Dutch oven.

GAME PLAN

1. Start the stew.
2. Make the biscuits.
3. Make a simple carrot salad with shredded carrots and raisins. Add your favorite low-fat coleslaw dressing.

SAVORY BEEF STEW

SERVES 4

¼   cup all-purpose flour
½   teaspoon salt
¼   teaspoon dry mustard
1   pound lean sirloin, trimmed of fat and cubed
1½   teaspoons olive oil
½   cup defatted beef broth
½   cups diced onions
2   tablespoons minced garlic
1   cup diced red potatoes
1   medium carrot, chopped

1 can (14 ounces) peeled whole tomatoes (with juice),
  chopped
2 tablespoons tomato paste
2 tablespoons balsamic vinegar
1 tablespoon brown sugar
1½ teaspoons dried thyme
2 bay leaves
  Salt and ground black pepper

Place the flour, salt, dry mustard and sirloin in a resealable plastic storage bag. Shake to combine. Heat the oil in a pressure cooker or heavy Dutch oven over medium-high heat. Transfer the beef to the pan, and brown on all sides.

Add the broth; bring to a boil, scraping the bottom of the pan to loosen any browned bits. Add the onions, garlic, potatoes, carrots, tomatoes (with juice), tomato paste, vinegar, brown sugar, thyme and bay leaves.

Lock the pressure cooker lid in place and bring to high pressure over high heat. Cook for 12 minutes. Release the pressure, and add salt and pepper to taste. Remove the bay leaves before serving.

Preparation time: 10 minutes
Cooking time: 15 minutes

Chef's note: If you don't have a pressure cooker, use a Dutch oven. Increase the amount of beef broth or water to 3 cups and cook for 1½ to 2 hours over medium heat, stirring occasionally.

Per serving: 333 calories, 7.4 g. fat (20% of calories), 4 g. dietary fiber, 65 mg. cholesterol, 599 mg. sodium.

CHIVE BISCUITS

MAKES 8

1¾ cups all-purpose flour
1 tablespoon baking powder
½ teaspoon baking soda
¼ teaspoon salt
1 tablespoon snipped fresh chives
2 tablespoons chilled margarine or butter
½ cup nonfat plain yogurt
⅓ cup low-fat buttermilk

Preheat the oven to 450°. In a food processor or large mixing bowl, combine the flour, baking powder, baking soda, salt and chives. Add the margarine or butter in small pieces; mix until the pastry is crumbly. Add the yogurt and buttermilk; mix just until the liquid is incorporated.

Drop the dough by large spoonfuls onto a 9″ × 13″ no-stick baking sheet. Bake for 12 minutes, or until lightly browned.

Preparation time: 8 minutes
Cooking time: 12 minutes

Per serving: 277 calories, 6.4 g. fat (21% of calories), 1.5 g. dietary fiber, 1 mg. cholesterol, 647 mg. sodium.

TURKEY TIME

Corn and Turkey Chowder
Green and White Bean Salad
French Bread

*W*ho needs cream and butter? Potatoes bring plenty of creamy richness to this thick soup. It's paired with a colorful bean salad that uses both fresh and canned beans, so it's a snap to make.

GAME PLAN

1. Make the chowder.
2. Make the salad and let it marinate.
3. Heat the French bread.

CORN AND TURKEY CHOWDER

SERVES 4

2¼	cups defatted chicken broth
1½	cups chopped onions
2	teaspoons chopped garlic
3	cups cubed cooked red potatoes
3½	cups frozen whole-kernel corn, thawed and drained
⅔	cup skim milk
½	cup diced cooked skinless turkey breast
	Salt and ground black pepper
¼	cup chopped fresh parsley

In a large soup pot over medium-high heat, heat ¼ cup of the broth; when it's simmering, add the onions. Cook and stir for 3 minutes, or until the onions are soft. Add the garlic, potatoes and remaining 2 cups of broth. Bring the soup to a boil. Simmer, covered, for 15 minutes, or until the potatoes are soft.

Puree half the corn in a blender. Add the pureed and whole corn, milk and turkey to the soup. Simmer for 15 minutes. Add salt and pepper to taste and stir in the parsley.

Preparation time: 10 minutes
Cooking time: 35 minutes

Per serving: 351 calories, 0.6 g. fat (1% of calories), 7.2 g. dietary fiber, 12 mg. cholesterol, 238 mg. sodium.

GREEN AND WHITE BEAN SALAD

SERVES 4

3 *cups diagonally sliced green beans*

1 *cup canned Great Northern beans, rinsed and drained*

2 *teaspoons olive oil*

¼ *cup minced fresh parsley*

¼ *cup minced fresh basil*

⅓ *cup balsamic vinegar*

2 *teaspoons honey mustard*

¼ *cup minced sweet or red onions*

½ *teaspoon salt*

   Ground black pepper

Bring a pot of water to a boil; add the green beans. Cook for 30 seconds, or until they turn bright green. Rinse under cold water and transfer to a medium bowl.

Add the Great Northern beans, oil, parsley, basil, vinegar, mustard and onions. Stir well. Let the salad marinate at room temperature for 30 minutes. Add the salt and pepper to taste.

Preparation time: 10 minutes
Cooking time: 30 seconds
Marinating time: 30 minutes

Per serving: 160 calories, 2.9 g. fat (16% of calories), 1.9 g. dietary fiber, no cholesterol, 295 mg. sodium.

FAST FIESTA

Mexican Chicken Tortilla Soup
Spicy Grilled Corn
Salsa
Sliced Avocados, Tomatoes and
Bell Peppers

This slightly spicy soup is perfect for an elegant summer dinner. The tortillas are cut into strips, then baked instead of fried. Add them to the soup just before serving. Grilled corn is cooked southwestern style, without the husks, for a chewy and flavorful side dish.

GAME PLAN

1. Start the soup.
2. Preheat the grill and prepare the corn for grilling.
3. Arrange a plate with tomatoes, sweet red or yellow bell peppers and a small amount of thinly sliced avocados.
4. Spoon the salsa into a bowl.
5. Bake the tortillas for the soup.
6. Grill the corn and finish the soup.

SPICY GRILLED CORN
SERVES 4

4	*large ears white or yellow corn on the cob, shucked*
1½	*teaspoons olive oil, warmed*
¼	*teaspoon ground cumin*
½	*teaspoon salt*
	Pinch of ground red pepper

Preheat the grill.

Place the corn, oil, cumin, salt and red pepper in a resealable plastic storage bag. Shake to combine.

Transfer the corn to the grill. Grill for 5 to 8 minutes, turning frequently, or until the corn is lightly browned, brushing the ears occasionally with any remaining oil.

Preparation time: 1 minute
Cooking time: 8 minutes

Per serving: 99 calories, 2.7 g. fat (22% of calories), 2.9 g. dietary fiber, no cholesterol, 280 mg. sodium.

•

MEXICAN CHICKEN TORTILLA SOUP

SERVES 4

   3   *cups defatted chicken broth*
  ½   *cup sliced onions*
   1   *cup diced red potatoes*
  ½   *large green pepper, diced*
   2   *teaspoons minced garlic*
   2   *boneless skinless chicken breast halves, cut into thin strips*
   1   *can (14 ounces) Mexican-style stewed tomatoes*
   1   *teaspoon chopped jalapeño peppers (wear plastic gloves when handling)*
  ½   *teaspoon ground cumin*
   4   *(6") corn tortillas*
   1   *tablespoon lime juice*
  ¼   *cup chopped fresh cilantro*

In a large soup pot over medium-high heat, bring ½ cup of the broth to a boil. Add the onions, potatoes, green peppers and garlic. Cook and stir for 5 minutes. Add the chicken; cook and stir for 1 minute.

Add the stewed tomatoes, jalapeño peppers, cumin and remaining 2½ cups of broth. Bring to a boil. Simmer the soup, uncovered, over medium heat for 15 minutes, or until the potatoes are soft.

Meanwhile, preheat the oven to 350°. Coat both sides of the tortillas with olive oil no-stick cooking spray; cut them into thin strips and place on a baking sheet. Bake for 15 minutes, or until crisp.

Add the lime juice and cilantro to the soup; top each bowl with the tortilla strips.

Preparation time: 10 minutes
Cooking time: 15 minutes

Per serving: 240 calories, 2.3 g. fat (8% of calories), 2.3 g. dietary fiber, 34 mg. cholesterol, 497 mg. sodium.

INDIAN SUMMER SUPPER

Butternut Squash Bisque
Red Pepper–Ricotta Bruschetta
Tossed Green Salad

This simple soup is a fast and delicious way to incorporate high-beta-carotene butternut squash into your meals. The "little toasts," or bruschetta, invented by thrifty Italian cooks, are a crunchy accompaniment.

GAME PLAN

1. Start the soup.
2. Make the bruschetta.
3. Make a simple tossed green salad from leaf lettuce, shredded red cabbage and sliced cucumbers. Add your favorite low-fat Italian dressing.
4. Puree the soup.

BUTTERNUT SQUASH BISQUE

SERVES 4

1	*large butternut squash*
1	*teaspoon olive oil*
2¼	*cups defatted chicken broth*
2	*teaspoons minced garlic*
2	*cups chopped onions*
1	*cup chopped sweet red peppers*
¼–½	*teaspoon ground red pepper*
½	*teaspoon ground cumin*
	Salt and ground black pepper
¼	*cup nonfat plain yogurt*

Pierce the squash several times with a sharp knife; place it on a paper towel in the microwave. Microwave on high for 5 minutes. Halve the squash lengthwise and remove the seeds; microwave on high for 5 more minutes.

In a large soup pot over medium-high heat, combine the olive oil and ¼ cup of the broth; bring to a boil. Add the garlic, onions and peppers; cook and stir for 5 minutes.

Scoop the squash from its shell and cut into chunks; add the squash, ground red pepper, cumin and remaining 2 cups of broth to the soup. Reduce the heat to medium. Bring to a boil; simmer, covered, for 15 minutes.

Transfer the soup to a blender or food processor; puree until smooth. Return the soup to the pot; heat through. Add salt and pepper to taste; garnish each serving with yogurt.

Preparation time: 10 minutes
Cooking time: 30 minutes

Per serving: 168 calories, 1.7 g. fat (8% total calories), 6 g. dietary fiber, 0.3 mg. cholesterol, 211 mg. sodium.

RED PEPPER–RICOTTA BRUSCHETTA

SERVES 4

8   *(¾") slices crusty French bread*
½   *cup light ricotta cheese*
2   *tablespoons nonfat mayonnaise*
2   *tablespoons nonfat plain yogurt*
2   *tablespoons grated Parmesan cheese*
½   *cup roasted sweet red peppers (from a jar), drained*

Toast the bread.

In a blender or bowl, combine the ricotta, mayonnaise, yogurt and Parmesan until smooth. Spread on the toasted bread.

Top each bruschetta with red peppers.

Preparation time: 10 minutes

Per serving: 191 calories, 3.4 g. fat (16% of calories), 0.5 g. dietary fiber, 7 mg. cholesterol, 486 mg. sodium.

POWWOW PARTY

Corn and Sweet Potato Stew
Toast with Low-Fat Pimento Cheese
Coleslaw

Inherited from Native American cooking, this delicious combination of fresh corn, tomatoes, chilies and sweet potatoes is a winner for winter months. The toast is topped with an old-fashioned favorite—pimento cheese—made lean with low-fat cheeses.

GAME PLAN

1. Make the stew.
2. Make the spread and refrigerate it.
3. Make a simple coleslaw from shredded red cabbage, shredded carrots and drained canned pineapple chunks. Add your favorite low-fat coleslaw dressing or nonfat plain yogurt.
4. Make the toast.

CORN AND SWEET POTATO STEW

SERVES 4

2½ *cups defatted chicken broth*
½ *cup chopped onions*
1 *tablespoon minced garlic*
1 *cup peeled and diced sweet potatoes*
1 *cup chopped sweet red peppers*
½ *cup diced zucchini or summer squash*
1 *cup whole-kernel corn*

1 can (14½ ounces) diced tomatoes with green chilies, or whole peeled tomatoes (with juice), chopped
1 cup cooked navy beans or brown rice
½ teaspoon dried thyme
1 teaspoon cornstarch
1 tablespoon dry sherry or apple juice
 Salt and ground black pepper
¼ cup low-fat sour cream

In a large soup pot over medium-high heat, bring ½ cup of the broth to a boil; add the onions. Cook and stir for 3 minutes. Add the garlic, sweet potatoes, peppers, zucchini or summer squash, corn, tomatoes (with juice), beans or rice and thyme. Cook and stir for 1 minute.

Add the remaining 2 cups of broth; bring to a boil. Reduce the heat to medium; simmer, covered, for 20 to 25 minutes, or until the sweet potatoes are tender.

In a small bowl, combine the cornstarch and sherry or apple juice; add to the stew. Cook and stir for 3 to 5 minutes, or until slightly thickened. Add salt and pepper to taste; garnish each bowl with sour cream.

Preparation time: 10 minutes
Cooking time: 30 minutes

Per serving: 281 calories, 1.9 g. fat (6% of calories), 7.5 g. dietary fiber, 5 mg. cholesterol, 574 mg. sodium.

TOAST WITH LOW-FAT PIMENTO CHEESE

4 ounces nonfat cream cheese
1 cup shredded low-fat sharp Cheddar cheese
⅓ cup light ricotta cheese
⅓ cup chopped, drained pimentos (from a jar)
¼ cup nonfat mayonnaise
⅓ cup plain nonfat yogurt
2 tablespoons minced red onions
8 slices reduced-sodium dark rye or whole-wheat bread

In a blender or food processor, combine the cream cheese, Cheddar and ricotta until smooth. Add the pimentos, mayonnaise and yogurt; process until the pimentos are finely chopped. Stir in the red onions. Transfer to a container and refrigerate for 15 minutes.

Toast the bread and cut it into triangles. Serve with the chilled spread.

Preparation time: 5 minutes
Chilling time: 15 minutes

Chef's note: Cube leftover toast as croutons for soup; leftover pimento cheese is great as a sandwich spread for lunch later in the week.

Per serving: 149 calories, 3.4 g. fat (18% of calories), no dietary fiber, 9 mg. cholesterol, 524 mg. sodium.

SIMPLY SCANDINAVIAN

Blender Potato Buttermilk Soup
Marinated Vegetable Salad
Rye Croutons

our blender and pressure cooker make this Scandinavian soup dinner almost instant. Low-fat buttermilk and potatoes thicken the creamy soup, and a crisp marinated salad adds plenty of vitamin-rich fresh vegetables.

GAME PLAN

1. Make the salad.
2. Make the soup.
3. Slice rye bread into strips, coat with olive oil no-stick cooking spray and bake for 15 minutes at 350°.

BLENDER POTATO BUTTERMILK SOUP

SERVES 4

1 *teaspoon olive oil*
1 *cup chopped onions*
3 *stalks celery, diced*
3 *medium baking potatoes, diced*
3 *cups defatted chicken broth*
2 *cups low-fat buttermilk*
¼ *cup sliced green onions*
  Salt and ground black pepper

Heat the oil in a pressure cooker over medium-high heat. Add the onions and celery; cook and stir for 2 minutes. Add the potatoes and broth. Lock the pressure cooker lid in place and bring to high pressure. Cook for 5 minutes. Remove the pressure cooker from the heat and release the pressure.

Transfer the soup to a blender or food processor; add the buttermilk and puree. Return the soup to the pot; heat through. Add the green onions and salt and pepper to taste.

Preparation time: 5 minutes
Cooking time: 7 minutes

Per serving: 263 calories, 2.5 g. fat (8% of calories), 5.1 g. dietary fiber, 5 mg. cholesterol, 420 mg. sodium.

MARINATED VEGETABLE SALAD

SERVES 4

½   cup thinly sliced red onions
1   cup diced cucumbers
½   cup sliced mushrooms
½   cup diced sweet red peppers
½   cup diced green peppers
2   tablespoons chopped fresh parsley
2   tablespoons lemon juice
2–3   tablespoons rice vinegar
2   teaspoons olive oil
1   teaspoon minced garlic
    Salt and ground black pepper
4   lettuce leaves

In a large bowl, combine the onions, cucumbers, mushrooms, red and green peppers, parsley, lemon juice, vinegar, oil and garlic. Add salt and pepper to taste. Let the salad marinate for 20 minutes at room temperature.

Line 4 salad plates with the lettuce leaves; arrange the salad on top of the lettuce.

Preparation time: 15 minutes
Marinating time: 20 minutes

Per serving: 59 calories, 2.6 g. fat (35% of calories), 1.7 g. dietary fiber, no cholesterol, 5 mg. sodium.

NEW MEXICO NIGHTS

Black Bean Stew with Smoked Turkey
Grilled Cheese Tortilla Wedges
Tossed Salad

This hearty menu of corn-and-black-bean stew and crisp tortillas can take the chill off any winter day. Smoked turkey and lean cheeses add high flavor without high fat.

GAME PLAN

1. Make the stew.
2. Make a simple tossed salad of canned artichoke hearts, romaine lettuce and sliced radishes. Add your favorite low-fat ranch dressing.
3. Make the tortilla wedges.

GRILLED CHEESE TORTILLA WEDGES

SERVES 4

¾   cup shredded low-fat Monterey Jack cheese
2   tablespoons thinly sliced green onions
¼   cup finely diced tomatoes
¼   cup nonfat sour cream
8   (8") flour tortillas

In a medium bowl, combine the Monterey Jack, green onions, tomatoes and sour cream. Divide between 4 tortillas, spreading evenly. Top with the remaining 4 tortillas.

Coat a 10" no-stick skillet with no-stick cooking spray; set it over medium-high heat. When the skillet is hot, cook the tortilla sandwiches for 3 to 4 minutes, or until the cheese has melted, turning once during cooking. Cut into wedges.

Preparation time: 5 minutes
Cooking time: 15 minutes

Per serving: 301 calories, 8.8 g. fat (27% of calories), 0.2 g. dietary fiber, 15 mg. cholesterol, 512 mg. sodium.

BLACK BEAN STEW WITH SMOKED TURKEY

SERVES 4

¼	cup dry sherry or apple juice
1	tablespoon olive oil
2	cups chopped onions
½	cup chopped celery
½	cup chopped carrots
½	cup chopped sweet red peppers
4	cups cooked black beans
2	ounces diced smoked lean turkey
2	cups whole-kernel corn
2	cups defatted chicken broth
2	tablespoons minced garlic
1	cup chopped tomatoes
2	teaspoons ground cumin
3–4	teaspoons chili powder
½	teaspoon dried oregano
¼	cup chopped fresh cilantro
2	tablespoons honey
2	tablespoons tomato paste

In a large soup pot over medium-high heat, combine the sherry or apple juice and oil; bring to a boil. Add the onions; cook and stir for 3 minutes, or until soft but not browned. Add the celery, carrots and peppers. Cook and stir for 5 minutes.

Add the beans, turkey, corn, broth, garlic, tomatoes, cumin, chili powder, oregano, cilantro, honey and tomato paste. Bring to a boil. Lower the heat to medium; simmer for 15 minutes.

Puree 1 cup of the stew in a blender, then return it to the pot.

Preparation time: 15 minutes
Cooking time: 25 minutes

Per serving: 495 calories, 5.6 g. fat (10% of calories), 13.4 g. dietary fiber, 6 mg. cholesterol, 432 mg. sodium.

New Down-Home Dinner

Pesto Chili
Cheesy Whole-Wheat Breadsticks
Fresh Fruit Plate

This rich-tasting pesto chili combines Texas heartiness with French flair. The crusty breadsticks are surprisingly quick—use a good-quality store-bought whole-wheat bread dough.

GAME PLAN

1. Make the chili.
2. Make the breadsticks.
3. Slice fresh fruit such as kiwifruit, pears, apples, melon and bananas. Arrange it on a platter.

CHEESY WHOLE-WHEAT BREADSTICKS

SERVES 4

2 *teaspoons cornmeal*
2 *tablespoons grated Parmesan cheese*
1 *tablespoon minced garlic*
¼ *teaspoon ground red pepper*
4 *ounces frozen whole-wheat bread dough, thawed*
1 *egg white, slightly beaten*

Preheat the oven to 450°. Line a baking sheet with parchment paper and sprinkle it with the cornmeal. Set aside.

In a large bowl, knead the cheese, garlic and red pepper into the dough. Form 8 balls. Roll each ball into a long breadstick; arrange on the baking sheet. Brush with beaten egg white.

Bake for 12 to 15 minutes, or until the breadsticks are crisp and golden brown.

Preparation time: 10 minutes
Cooking time: 15 minutes

Per serving: 106 calories, 2.4 g. fat (21% of calories), 0.3 g. dietary fiber, 4 mg. cholesterol, 210 mg. sodium.

PESTO CHILI

SERVES 4

¼ cup water

1 teaspoon olive oil

1 cup chopped onions

2 teaspoons minced garlic

1 cup diced red potatoes

1 cup diced carrots or peeled winter squash

½ cup chopped celery leaves

2 cups canned chopped tomatoes (with juice)

2 cups canned reduced-sodium kidney beans, drained

2 cups defatted reduced-sodium chicken broth

2 teaspoons reduced-sodium tomato paste

2 tablespoons minced fresh parsley

2 teaspoons dried basil

1 cup chopped fresh spinach leaves

2 teaspoons toasted pine nuts

¼ cup grated Parmesan cheese

In a large soup pot over medium-high heat, bring the water and oil to a boil. Add the onions and 1 teaspoon of the garlic. Cook and stir for 5 to 6 minutes, or until the onions are soft but not browned.

Add the potatoes, carrots or squash, celery leaves, tomatoes (with juice) and beans. Cook and stir for 2 minutes. Add the broth and tomato paste; bring to a boil. Cover and simmer over medium heat for 15 minutes, or until the potatoes are soft.

In a blender or food processor, combine the parsley, basil, spinach, pine nuts and Parmesan; puree. Stir into the soup.

Preparation time: 10 minutes
Cooking time: 25 minutes

Per serving: 299 calories, 6 g. fat (17% of calories), 10.8 g. dietary fiber, 6 mg. cholesterol, 161 mg. sodium.

SUPER STEW SUPPER

Chick-Pea and Pasta Stew
Cheddar Corn Muffins
Cucumber Salad

Salad bar vegetables make this stew quick to prepare. The muffins are rich-tasting without the fat; applesauce and low-fat buttermilk lighten the batter.

GAME PLAN

1. Make the muffins.
2. Make the stew.
3. Make a simple salad of sliced cucumbers, chopped green onions, minced red onions, rice vinegar and a drizzle of honey. Arrange it on lettuce leaves.

CHEDDAR CORN MUFFINS

MAKES 12

  1   *cup unbleached all-purpose flour*
 ¼   *cup cornmeal*
  1   *teaspoon baking powder*
 ½   *teaspoon baking soda*
 ½   *teaspoon salt*
 ½   *cup shredded low-fat sharp Cheddar cheese*
 ½   *cup shredded bran cereal*
 ¾   *cup low-fat buttermilk*
  2   *tablespoons canola oil or softened butter*
  2   *tablespoons unsweetened applesauce*
  1   *large egg*
 ⅓   *cup maple syrup*
 ½   *cup whole-kernel corn*

Preheat the oven to 400°. Lightly oil and flour a 12-cup muffin tin. Set aside.

In a large mixing bowl, combine the flour, cornmeal, baking powder, baking soda and salt. Add the Cheddar and cereal; toss to coat. In another bowl, whisk together the buttermilk, oil or butter, applesauce, egg, maple syrup and corn. Combine the contents of both bowls, folding just until the dry ingredients are moistened. Spoon the batter into the muffin tin.

Bake for 15 to 20 minutes, or until the muffins are golden brown and springy to the touch, and a toothpick inserted in the center of one muffin comes out clean.

Preparation time: 10 minutes
Cooking time: 20 minutes

Per muffin: 123 calories, 3.8 g. fat (26% of calories), 1.7 g. dietary fiber, 21 mg. cholesterol, 276 mg. sodium.

FAST FROM THE FREEZER: INSTANT SOUP IDEAS

On really busy nights, there's always soup for dinner. Each of these tasty concoctions can be put together in less than 10 minutes—with ingredients from your freezer and pantry shelves.

• **Spicy Mexican Soup:** In a 10″ no-stick skillet over medium-high heat, combine 2 cups frozen mixed vegetables, ½ cup medium salsa, 1 teaspoon olive oil and 1 teaspoon chopped mild green chili peppers (wear plastic gloves when handling); cook and stir for 5 minutes. Add 3 cups defatted chicken broth and 1 cup chopped cooked boneless, skinless chicken; bring to a boil. Cook for 5 minutes, stirring occasionally. Add salt and ground black pepper to taste. Serve with nonfat sour cream and chopped fresh cilantro. Serves 4.

• **Boffo Beef and Vegetable Soup:** Trim excess fat from 3 ounces frozen sirloin steak; cut it into small pieces. Dredge the beef in flour. In a medium saucepan over medium-high heat, combine 1 cup frozen mixed vegetables, 1 teaspoon olive oil, ¼ teaspoon ground cumin and the beef; cook and stir for 5 minutes, or until the beef is no longer pink in the center. Add 2 cups defatted beef stock, 1 cup reduced-sodium tomato sauce and salt and ground black pepper to taste; bring to a boil. Cook and stir for 5 minutes. Serves 4.

CHICK-PEA AND PASTA STEW

SERVES 4

  1   teaspoon olive oil
 ¼   cup dry red wine or red grape juice
  1   cup chopped onions
  2   cloves garlic, minced
  1   cup chopped tomatoes
 ⅓   cup chopped fresh parsley
 ⅓   cup frozen sliced carrots
 ⅓   cup chopped celery
 ½   cup cooked and diced red potatoes
  1   cup cooked macaroni
  1   cup canned chick-peas, drained
  4   cups defatted chicken broth
  2   teaspoons dried basil
 ¼   teaspoon dried oregano
 ½   teaspoon dried chives
      Salt and ground black pepper

In a large soup pot over medium-high heat, combine the oil and red wine or grape juice; bring to a boil. Add the onions; cook for 5 minutes, or until soft but not browned. Add the garlic, tomatoes, parsley, carrots and celery. Cook and stir for 5 minutes.

Add the potatoes, macaroni, chick-peas, broth, basil, oregano and chives; bring to a boil. Lower the heat to medium and cook, uncovered, for 15 minutes, or until the vegetables are soft.

Puree 1 cup of the stew in a blender or food processor, then return it to the pot. Add salt and pepper to taste.

Preparation time: 15 minutes
Cooking time: 25 minutes

Per serving: 211 calories, 2.8 g. fat (11% of calories), 5.8 g. dietary fiber, no cholesterol, 598 mg. sodium.

BETTER BREAD SPREADS

• **Bagels with Sweet Ricotta Spread:** Toast 2 halved bagels. In a small bowl, mash together ⅓ cup low-fat ricotta cheese, 2 tablespoons finely chopped dates and 1 tablespoon honey. Spread over the toasted bagels. Serves 4.

• **Pita Wedges with Chick-Pea Spread:** Toast 4 pita rounds in a toaster oven for 2 minutes, then cut them with scissors into 6 to 8 wedges each. In a small bowl, mash 1 cup cooked chick-peas with ¼ cup low-fat mayonnaise or nonfat plain yogurt and 2 tablespoons honey mustard. Season to taste with salt, pepper and celery seed. Use as a dip for the pita wedges. Serves 4.

• **Whole-Wheat Hamburger Buns with Japanese Tofu Spread:** Split and toast 2 whole-wheat hamburger buns. In a small bowl or food processor, cream 4 ounces drained soft tofu, 1 teaspoon tahini or peanut butter, 1 tablespoon reduced-fat mayonnaise, 1 tablespoon miso and 1 teaspoon minced black olives. Add lemon juice, salt and pepper to taste. Spread on the toasted buns. Serves 4.

• **Tortilla Wraps with Spicy Bean Spread:** Wrap 4 whole-wheat tortillas in plastic wrap and microwave for 1 minute on high power to warm. In a small bowl, mash 1½ cups canned black beans, drained, with 1 tablespoon lemon juice, 1 teaspoon chili powder, 2 tablespoons spicy salsa, a pinch of ground cumin and 1 teaspoon minced garlic. Add salt and pepper to taste. Spoon onto the tortillas and roll up. Serves 4.

• **Creamy Banana Spread on Toast:** Toast 2 to 4 slices of rye or whole-wheat bread. In a small bowl, mash together ½ ripe banana, 4 ounces reduced-fat cream cheese, 1 teaspoon lemon juice and 1 teaspoon honey. Stir in ¼ cup raisins and spread on the toast. Serves 4.

Savory Beef Stew (page 34)

Butternut Squash Bisque (page 42) and Red Pepper–Ricotta Bruschetta (page 43)

Curried Chick-Peas (page 68)

Black Bean and Corn Salad (page 79)